HE SHE THEY

THAT IS THE QUESTION—

GOD'S ANSWER

TERIE BRADFORD

outskirts
press

Outskirts Press, Inc.
http://www.outskirtspress.com

ISBN: 978-1-9772-2099-8

Outskirts Press and the "OP" logo are trademarks belonging to Outskirts Press, Inc.

PRINTED IN THE UNITED STATES OF AMERICA

Reasons for this book were Inspired by:

Joe Biden — Politician

> "We are in the battle for America's soul. –We have to choose truth over lies. America is coming back like it used to be: ethical, straight, telling the truth.

Pete Buttigieg — Mayor of South Bend, Indiana

> "We live in a moment that compels us each to act."

Tony Katz — WIBC Host

> "If you want to beat someone –
> beat them on the merits."

Donald Trump —

> "Make America Great Again!!!"

Jesus Christ — God's son

> "If you should abide by my words,
> truly you are my disciples. And you
> will know the truth and that truth will
> set you free."

We are still struggling to answer the age old cosmic questions:

Why am I here?

Why was I born?

Does my life have a purpose?

Is there a GOD?

If there is a God – why would he care about me?

What would he expect of me?

Just like everyone else, I have asked these questions throughout my life. Studying the Bible, I have found the answers. They are spelled out clear as day. Do not take mine, or anyone else's word – study for yourself, as I have. My studies have formed very strong opinions in my soul. Many will agree with me – some may not. But God's word is undisputable. People will ask me what I think about this or that – I say it is not your opinion or mine that matters — only God's. This world, and this life, is all about him – not you or me. You MUST study to understand him. The whole earth and our past screams it's HIStory.

We were created to worship him – to be a companion. He delighted in creating the world and Adam and Eve. I believe our fall was a great disappointment to him. But, individually, we can make up for that to him – one on one.

Please note: It is not my place to judge anyone who has not come to Christ. That belongs solely to God. For only God knows a man's heart and inner thoughts and motives. My goal with this book it to shine the light on God's word. The truth will set you free!! This is not just a trite statement – it is a living thing. Just get his word into your heart and soul. As the Bible says: "To whom much is forgiven, much is required." What inspiring words. With God, we are all on equal ground. He is not a respecter of persons. We are all sinners:

Romans 3:23 – yes, all have sinned; all fall short of God's glorious ideal; yet now God declares us "Not guilty" of offending him if we trust in Jesus Christ, who in his kindness freely takes away our sins.

The definitive word is 'if'. It is indeed time to rise up and stand for the truth. But, what is the truth? How do you find it?

John 18:37 Pilate askes Jesus: "Are you a king?"

Jesus replies: "Yes. I was born for that purpose. And I came to bring truth to the world. All who love the truth are my followers." Pilate asks: " What is the truth?"

1 Corinthians 1:18 - I know very well how foolish it sounds to those who are lost, when they hear that Jesus died to save them. But we who are saved recognize this message as the very power of God. For God says, "I will destroy all human plans of salvation no matter how wise they seem to be, and ignore the best ideas of men, even the most brilliant of them."

1 Corinthians 1:20 - So what about these wise men, these scholars, these brilliant debaters of this world's great affairs? God has made them all look foolish and shown

their wisdom to be useless nonsense. For God in his wisdom saw to it that the world would never find God through human brilliance, and then he stepped in and saved all those who believed his message, which the world calls foolish and silly.

1 Corinthians 1:26 - Notice among yourselves, dear brothers, that few of you who follow Christ have big names or power or wealth. Instead, God has deliberately chosen to use ideas the world considers foolish and of little worth in order to shame those people considered by the world as wise and great. He has chosen a plan despised by the world, counted as nothing at all, and used it to bring down to nothing those the world considers great, so that no one anywhere can ever brag in the presence of God.

1 Corinthians 2:14 - In telling you about these gifts we have even used the very words given to us by the Holy Spirit, not words that we as men might choose. So we use the Holy Spirit's words to explain the Holy Spirit's facts. But the man who isn't a Christian can't understand and can't accept these thoughts from God, which the Holy Spirit teaches us. They sound foolish to him because only those who have the Holy Spirit within them can understand what the Holy Spirit means. Others just can't take it in.

John 16:13 - When the Holy Spirit, who is truth, comes, he shall guide you into all truth, for he will not be presenting his own ideas, but will be passing on to you what he has heard. He will tell you about the future. He shall praise me and bring me great honor by showing you my glory.

All the Father's glory is mine; this is what I mean when I say that he will show you my glory.

The Bible will answer all your questions for you – but it takes dedication, work and study.

2 Timothy 2:15 – Study to shew thyself approved unto God. A workman that needeth not to be ashamed, rightly dividing the word of truth.

This is not an easy task. It may take you most of your life. God gives us this life to work through our salvation.

Pilippians 2:12 – Work out your own salvation with fear and trembling.

Hebrews 10:31 – It is a fearful thing to fall into the hands of the living God.

Romans 14:10 – But why dost thou judge thy brother? Or, why dost thy set at naught thy brother? For we shall all stand before the judgment seat of Christ.

Romans 14:11 – For it is written: As I live, saith the LORD, every knee shall bow to me and every tongue shall confess to God. So then, every one of us shall give account of himself to God.

Yes, we will all die and be judged by God someday. This earthly life is just our proving ground. Notice it says; "All" – that means individually – each one of us. We cannot, as much as we might want to, answer for anyone else – we stand alone!!! Know that God knows you – your inner self, your strengths and weaknesses – your past sorrows – your joys. He has been with you since he created you. Why does he love you & care about YOU? Just as any creator cares about what they have made. God is watching you to see what you will do with his creation. He has given you your attributes, intelligence, a drive to become. He created the being – now he is watching you become!!! And hoping that you come to the conclusion, that the creator is greater than the creation. What an awesome idea to absorb! There is no lying or hiding from God. He is always with you.

Ecclesiastes 12:14 – For God shall bring out every work into judgement, with every secret thing, whether it be good or whether it be evil.

Jeremiah 23:24 – Can any hide himself in secret places that I shall not see him? Saith the Lord. Do not I fill heaven and

earth? Saith the Lord.

Hear ye!!! Hear ye!!! Let it be known! Let it be shouted! God is a forgiving God! He loves you soooo much! He will forgive the vilest of sins. All you have to do is repent of them and come to him with a contrite heart. Believe me, I have been forgiven much. Like Allen Jackson says: "I am a work in progress." I am always reminded of the man who told Jesus he had never broken a commandment. This blows my mind! As I have broken almost all of them. — covetousness, stealing, adultery, murder, breaking the Sabbath, honoring my parents. Even with all this bad, I have always loved the Lord. Read Luke 18:18

You must have a healthy fear of God:

Luke 12 : 4 - "Dear friends, don't be afraid of these who want to murder you. They

can only kill the body; they have no power over your souls. But I'll tell you whom to fear—fear God who has the power to kill and then cast into hell.

Romans 5:6 - When we were utterly helpless, with no way of escape, Christ came at just the right time and died for us sinners who had no use for him. Even if we were good, we really wouldn't expect anyone to die for us, though, of course, that might be barely possible. But God showed his great love for us by sending Christ to die for us while we were still sinners. And since by his blood he did all this for us as sinners, how much more will he do for us now that he has declared us not guilty? Now he will save us from all of God's wrath to come. And since, when we were his enemies, we were brought back to God by the death of his Son, what

blessings he must have for us now that we are his friends and he is living within us!

My favorite verse in the whole Bible:

Romans 10:43 – For whosover shall call upon the name of the Lord shall be saved.

That verse is so precious to me. It solidifies God's love, mercy and grace. I am that whosover – so are you. So no, as I write this – believe in your heart of hearts that I do not judge you for your sin (not my place) – but also know that God will. His salvation comes with a great responsibility. We have to turn away from sin – recognize it for what it is. Realize that with God's help we can face our sins – turn away from them and repent and return to God. We cannot claim to love God and remain in our sins. This is why he sent his only begotten son to die a horrible death to redeem us. With his blood on us, God sees us as his dear children and smiles at us. Just as we do with our own children after we forgive them for an error.

John 3:16 - For God loved the world so much that he gave his only Son.........so that anyone who believes in him shall not perish but have eternal life. God did not send his Son into the world to condemn it, but to save it.

Notice God sent his ONLY son to die for us. What a greater sacrifice then coming himself. How much harder to ask your precious son to die for someone – than yourself!!

Psalm 103:8 The lord is merciful and gracious, slow to anger, and plenteous in mercy. He will not always chide: neither will he keep his anger forever. He hath not

dealt with us after our sins; nor rewarded us according to our iniquities. For as the heaven is high above the earth, so great is his mercy toward them that fear him. As far as the east is from the west, so far hath he removed our transgressions from us. Like as a father pitieth his children, so the lord pitieth them that fear him. For he knoweth our frame; he remembereth that we are dust.

Galatians 6:5 - For every man shall bear his own burden. Let him that is taught in the word communicate unto him that teacheth in all good things. Be not deceived; God is not mocked: for whatsoever a man soweth, that shall he also reap. For he that soweth to his flesh shall of the flesh reap corruption; but he that soweth to the Spirit shall of the Spirit reap life everlasting.

Beware! – this forgiveness is only for those covered by the blood. Only by accepting Jesus and his deity, sacrifice, and love, can we come to God after death as his beloved child. Those dying in their sins and not accepting Christ will burn in hell eternally.

BORN ONCE – DIE TWICE

BORN TWICE – DIE ONCE

For we have to be "born again" to enter the kingdom of Heaven as his child. A spiritual birth. Thus, we can't suffer the eternal death. We will be given eternal life. What a glorious day that will be!

The big cosmic question is: Is there a God? Was Jesus really God's son?

Many books have been written on this subject. Read as many as you can. That said, I see no reason to "reinvent the wheel".

446

I think it is really funny when I hear people talk about the Big Bang theory – Duh! What do you think creation was? Read Fred Hoyle ...... a fine tuning - requires a fine tuner!!! He discovered the conditions required to create carbon, and the minute likelihood of this happening by chance. I believe it is one of the best proofs of creation. But there are so many more – study to show yourself approved!

Stephen Hawking: "The remarkable fact is that the values of these numbers seem to have been very finely adjusted to make possible the development of life."

****Houston – we have a problem!!! Science has proven intelligent design – or creation!!! Just study photosynthesis, oxygen, light (gamma rays, xrays, ultraviolet, etc.), our atmosphere that blocks the bad stuff from killing us and lets the life building light in. Study our DNA – the cell, bacterial flagellum (with it's motor – stator, rotor, u-joint, drive shaft, propeller). Chemicals that produce code – digital characters that direct construction of proteins for us to stay alive. Then ask yourself – could this have all happened without intelligence or a creator?? Creation, dinosaurs, dragons, fossils, the universe, the stars, the seasons —the air we breathe – it's all in the Bible! Do not choose to be willfully ignorant. Again – study! Read Stephen Meyer and Bijan Nemati.

Just look around at nature. Proof of God's sense of humor is seen in the Birds of Paradise – or look at the pictures The Hubble sends us. Who else but God could imagine such a thing! There are a lot of books and videos proving creation – just study.

About Jesus – again so many books and proofs – but one thing I say to people:

"I have to tell you about a dream I had about you. It was so real! I dreamt that another company much like the one you are working for – a competitor – called you and offered you a job. No weekends and twice your current salary!" Now .... What would you think if a few days later it came true and you accepted the new job! My prediction came true! You would think I was incredible." This is what happened with Jesus – only with over 100 predictions - over a period of approx. 2500BC to 400BC - years before his birth. By people who had never heard of each other, lived years apart, living in different places – without a computer or a phone or the internet!! Every prophecy was fulfilled by his life. Some were very bold ie: born of a virgin — some were quite obscure: ride on a donkey. Point is, there are many proofs that he lived and was indeed God's son. This fact cannot be disputed. Read about archaeology – there have been many discoveries proving the Bible is correct. Get a subscription to Biblical Archaeology Review - Study! Also he was seen resurrected by over 500 people. People were martyred who believed in him. Why would someone go to their death for something they did not deeply believe to be true?

Stephen

Acts 6 and 7 give us the account of Stephen's martyrdom. Stephen is considered one of the first Christian martyrs after Christ himself.

Stephen was speaking the truth of Jesus

Christ. However, his words offended the listeners. They put together a council that brought false-witness to the things Stephen was saying (Acts 6:11-13). Stephen proclaimed that God's own people were at fault for suppressing the prophets' call to righteousness. They even killed the Holy One, Jesus Christ.

Their reaction was to gnash on him with their teeth. They ran Stephen out of the city and stoned him. Yet Stephen patiently accepted the persecution that was given to him. Stephen asked the Lord not to hold them guilty who had stoned him. He essentially repeated Christ's words on the cross. "Forgive them, for they know not what they do."

Andrew

Andrew was one of the first disciples of Christ. He was previously a disciple of John (John 1:40). Andrew was the brother of the boisterous Simon Peter. After the biblical record of Andrew's life, he went on to preach around the Black Sea and was influential in starting several churches. He was the founder of the church in Byzantium or Constantinople.

Tradition says that Andrew was crucified on an X shaped cross on the northern coast of Peloponnese. Early writings state that the cross was actually a Latin cross like the one Jesus was crucified upon. But the traditional story says that Andrew refused to be crucified in the same manner as Christ because he was not worthy.

Simon Peter

Brought to Christ by his brother Andrew, Peter is known as the disciple who spoke often before he thought. After Christ's death Peter was the fiery preacher prominently seen in the first half of the book of Acts. He founded the church at Antioch and traveled preaching mainly to Jews about Jesus Christ.

Peter was martyred under Nero's reign. He was killed in Rome around the years 64 to 67. Tradition holds that he was crucified upside down. Like Andrew, his brother, he is said to have refused to be crucified in the same manner as Christ because he was unworthy to be executed in the same way as the Lord.

Polycarp

As with many people in the early centuries, Polycarp's exact birth and death dates are not known. Even his date of martyrdom is disputed; though it was some time between AD 155 and 167. Polycarp was probably a disciple of the Apostle John who wrote the books of the Gospel of John, the three Epistles of John and the book of Revelation. Polycarp may have been one of the chief people responsible for compiling the New Testament of the Bible that we have today.

Because of his refusal to burn incense to the Roman Emperor he was sentenced to burn at the stake. Tradition says that the flames did not kill him so he was stabbed to death.

Wycliffe

Known as "The Morning Star of the Reformation," John Wycliffe was a 14th century theologian. He is probably best remembered as a translator of scriptures. He believed that the Bible should be available to the people in their common tongue. He translated the Latin Vulgate into common English.

He was persecuted for his stand against Papal authority. While he was not burned at the stake as a martyr, his persecution extended beyond his death. His body was exhumed and burned along with many of his writings. The Anti-Wycliffe Statute of 1401 brought persecution to his followers and specifically addressed the fact that there should not be any translation of Scripture into English.

John Huss

Huss was a Czech priest who was burned at the stake for heresy against the doctrines of the Catholic Church. Particularly he fought against the doctrines of Ecclesiology and the Eucharist as taught by the Roman Catholic Church. He was an early reformer living before the time of Luther and Calvin (other well-known reformers of Roman Catholicism).

Huss was martyred on July 6, 1415. He refused to recant his position of the charges that were brought against him. On the day he died he is said to have stated, *"God is my witness that the things charged against me I never preached. In the same truth of the Gospel which I have written, taught, and preached, drawing upon the sayings and positions of the holy doctors, I am ready to die today."*

William Tyndale

Most known for his translation of the Bible into English, William Tyndale was a reformer who stood against many teachings of the Catholic Church and opposed King Henry VIII's divorce, which was one of the major issues in the Reformation. Tyndale's English translation of the Bible was the first to draw significantly from the original languages.

Tyndale was choked to <u>death</u> while tied to the stake and then his dead body was burned. The date of commemoration of Tyndale's martyrdom is October 6, 1536 but he probably died a few weeks earlier than that.

Jim Elliot and Four Missionary Friends

Jim Elliot, along with four of his missionary colleagues was killed on January 8,

1956 while trying to establish contact with the Auca Indians in Ecuador (now known as the Waodani people). Jim Elliot, Nate Saint, Ed McCully, Pete Flemming and Roger Youderian had been working to make friendly contact with the Auca tribe which they had seen from the air. Though they had only met one tribesman face to face, they had participated in trades with the Auca from a plane to ground system. When Elliot and his friends landed on a river beach on that fateful January day they were slaughtered by the waiting men.

Their deaths were not in vain though. The widows continued to try and make peaceful contact and eventually won the hearts of the tribe. God has used this recent missionary martyr story to inspire new generations of missionaries willing to give their lives for what they believe.

Nag Hammadi Massacre

On the night of January 7, 2010 a group of eight Egyptian Christians were killed as they left their church after celebrating a Christmas mass in Nag Hammadi, Egypt. The motive behind the massacre is disputed, but it was carried out by militant Islamic believers. It may have been done in retaliation for an alleged crime against a Muslim girl by a Christian man. Even if that was the reason, the retaliation was not targeted at the man who committed the crime but at Christians because of their association through religion.

This type of martyrdom happens in many parts of the world today. There are still wars being fought on small and large scales because Christians hold strongly to their beliefs. The Christians are not the aggressors in most cases. They are being targeted be-cause of their religion.

Christian Martyrdom

It is heartbreaking to see anyone killed for any reason. However, Christians through the centuries have been tenacious in hold-ing to their beliefs. While 10 martyrs or groups of martyrs were mentioned here, there are many more you can read about. One great book to get you started on your study of Christian martyrs is the classic book, Foxe's Book of Martyrs.

Read more: https://www.whatchristian-swanttoknow.com/10-famous-christian-martyrs/#ixzz62H1dTimo

Why would soooo many people through-out the ages suffer insults and death for Jesus if there was not a deep love for him?

Pray for guidance when you study. I pray that you will grow to love the LORD this much! God wants you to know him. With God there are no gray areas – only black and white. He does not want us confused. He even warns us against false prophets and teachers. There is no way you can read the Bible and misunderstand what he is saying. He wants us all to accept him and live forever with him – in the place he will prepare for us. Pray for God to shine his light on your wrongs:

Psalm 139: 23 - Search me, O God, and know my heart; test my thoughts. Point out anything you find in me that makes you sad, and lead me along the path of everlasting life.

John 14:1 – Jesus said: Let not your heart be troubled: ye believe in God, believe

also in me. In my Father's house are many mansions: if it were not so, I would have told you. I go to prepare a place for you. And if I go and prepare a place for you, I will come again, and receive you unto myself; that where I am, there ye may be also.

So, we know God loves us and Jesus died for our sins – so we can go boldly before the throne of God:

Hebrews 4:15-16 - For we have not an high priest which cannot be touched with the feeling of our infirmities; but was in all points tempted like as we are, yet without sin. Let us therefore come boldly unto the throne of grace, that we may obtain mercy, and find grace to help in time of need.

As Jesus told the woman who was going to be stoned for adultery: " go and sin no more". (John 8 – read this story!) Once we accept God and his son – it is our responsibility to study and to learn his will for our lives and how we are to conduct ourselves, so we can avoid sin.

I once had a friend ask me for advice. She said she had two job offers and was not sure which one to accept. I said I don't think God cares whether you are a doctor or a janitor. Whichever job would make you the happiest is what he would want for you – just like any good father. He only cares about your heart – that you do the job with joy, integrity and honesty. He wants our focus on higher things.

So, God does not care what kind of car you drive – or if one – or where you live, what race or nationality you are. He wants us to live godly lives and to be a blessing to those around us. This is our main purpose. To worship him.

So, we come full circle – back to sin – it separates us from God. But what is sin? Just the 10 commandments? No, the Bible teaches us it is also immorality.

The Ten Commandments:

1. You shall have no other gods before Me.

2. You shall make no idols.

3. You shall not take the name of the Lord your God in vain.

4. Keep the Sabbath day holy.

5. Honor your father and your mother.

6. You shall not murder.

7. You shall not commit adultery.

8. You shall not steal.

9. You shall not bear false witness against your neighbor.

10. You shall not covet.

It is the BIG lie of today that homosexuality is OK. It is not. It is a sin. If you care at all for God and have any desire to live eternally, you must deny it. Unfortunately, many politicians and even church leaders are helping to promote the Devil's lie – for their own agenda and greed.

Leviticus 18:22 - Homosexuality is absolutely forbidden, for it is an enormous sin.

it is abomination.

Leviticus 20:13 – The penalty for homosexual acts is death to both parties. They

have brought it upon themselves.

Romans 1:22 - Professing themselves to be wise, they became fools, And changed the glory of the uncorruptible God into an image made like to corruptible man, and to birds, and fourfooted beasts, and creeping things. Wherefore God also gave them up to uncleanness through the lusts of their own hearts, to dishonour their own bodies between themselves: Who changed the truth of God into a lie, and worshipped and served the creature more than the Creator, who is blessed for ever. Amen.

For this cause God gave them up unto vile affections: for even their women did change the natural use into that which is against nature: And likewise also the men, leaving the natural use of the woman, burned in their lust one toward another; men with men working that which is unseemly, and receiving in themselves that recompence of their error which was meet.

And even as they did not like to retain God in their knowledge, God gave them over to a reprobate mind, to do those things which are not convenient;

Being filled with all unrighteousness, fornication, wickedness, covetousness, maliciousness; full of envy, murder, debate, deceit, malignity; whisperers,

Backbiters, haters of God, despiteful, proud, boasters, inventors of evil things, disobedient to parents, Without understanding, covenant breakers, without natural affection, implacable, unmerciful:

Who knowing the judgment of God, that they which commit such things are worthy of death, not only do the same, but have pleasure in them that do them.

1 Corinthians 6:10 - -Don't you know that those doing such things have no share in the Kingdom of God? Don't fool yourselves. Those who live immoral lives, who are idol worshipers, adulterers or homosexuals—will have no share in his Kingdom. Neither will thieves or greedy people, drunkards, slanderers, or robbers. There was a time when some of you were just like that but now your sins are washed away, and you are set apart for God; and he has accepted you because of what the Lord Jesus Christ and the Spirit of our God have done for you.

1 Timothy 1:18 - Those laws are good when

used as God intended. But they were not made for us, whom God has saved; they are for sinners who hate God, have rebellious hearts, curse and swear, attack their fathers and mothers, and murder. Yes, these laws are made to identify as sinners all who are immoral and impure: homosexuals, kidnappers, liars, and all others who do things that contradict the glorious Good News of our blessed God, whose messenger I am.

This is today's battleground. God created us male or female – not our choice – God, as the creator made us just the way he wanted us. I believe as far as the Bible is concerned you can lump any behavior besides following the way you were created as homosexual. He loves variety. He is not a cookie cutter creator! He made you unique – for a purpose. He gives us all gifts of the spirit.

1 Corinthians 12:4 - And there are diversities of gifts, and the same Spirit;

and there are diversities of ministrations, and the same Lord;

and there are diversities of workings, and it is the same God -- who is working the all in all.

And to each hath been given the manifestation of the Spirit for profit;

for to one through the Spirit hath been given a word of wisdom, and to another a word of knowledge, according to the same Spirit;

and to another faith in the same Spirit, and to another gifts of healings in the same Spirit;

and to another in-workings of mighty deeds; and to another prophecy; and to another discernings of spirits; and to another [divers] kinds of tongues; and to another interpretation of tongues:

and all these doth work the one and the same Spirit, dividing to each severally as he intendeth.

He created YOU for a reason. Find yours and live for him!

Jeremiah 1:5 - I knew you before you were formed within your mother's womb; before you were born I sanctified you...

God would never create someone gay. It is not possible. Some people try to claim this – but God cannot look on sin & it would be against his nature to do so. This is a lie the devil uses – he wants you bad!

But not as bad as God wants YOU!!!! The devil is using people for his agenda and unfortunately even people professing to be Christian are perverting his word for their own desires and to get ahead. You can never trust someone who is so deceiving. Do not believe them – follow God and his word. They will get their comeupends! AGAIN — STUDY.

Through this, there is a great perversion and molesting of our nation's soul and people. It is an affront to all true Christians to legitimize sin. Any sin. Is it OK to commit adultery, to rob someone, to murder? God says sin is sin. No gray. As Joe Biden pointed out, we are losing America's soul. Our forefathers and leaders founded this country on God's word:

William Penn

"Those who will not be governed by God will be ruled by tyrants."

As recently as 1952 Justice William O. Douglas wrote:

"We are a religious people whose institutions presuppose a Supreme Being."

George Washington wrote a prayer addressed to "O most glorious God, in Jesus Christ" and ended it like this:

"... Let me live according to those holy rules which Thou hast this day prescribed in Thy holy word ... Direct me to the true object, Jesus Christ the way, the truth and the life. Bless, O Lord, all the people of this land."

"Reason and experience both forbid us to

expect that national morality can prevail in exclusion of religious principle."

"It is impossible to rightly govern . . . without God & the Bible."

"You do well to wish to learn our arts and ways of life, and above all the religion of Jesus Christ." to a group of Indian chiefs.

John Adams wrote:

"Our Constitution was made only for a moral and religious people. It is wholly inadequate to the government of any other."

"We have no government armed with power capable of contending with passions unbridled by morality and religion."

"Religion & virtue are the only foundations, not only of republicanism and of all free government, but of social felicity under all governments and in all the combinations of human society."

"Statesmen, my dear sir, may plan and speculate for liberty, but it is religion and morality alone, which can establish the principles upon which freedom can securely stand."

Thomas Jefferson, the man "blamed" for the wall of separation between church and state said:

"I have always said, and will always say, that the studious perusal of the sacred volume will make us better citizens."

"And can the liberties of a nation be thought secure when we have removed their only firm basis, a conviction in the minds of the people that these liberties are the gift of God? That they are not to be violated but with His wrath? Indeed, I tremble for my country when I reflect that God is just: that His justice cannot sleep forever."

"No power over the freedom of religion . . .[is] delegated to the United States by the Constitution."

"Of all the systems of morality, ancient or modern, which have come under my observation, none appears to me so pure as that of Jesus."

"I am a Christian, in the only sense in which he wished any one to be; sincerely attached to his doctrines, in preference to all others; ascribing to himself every human excellence; and believing he never claimed any other." Letter to Benjamin Rush, April 21, 1803

James Madison:

"We have staked the whole future of American civilization, not on the power of government...[but] upon the capacity of each and every one of us to govern ourselves according to the Ten Commandments of God."

"Before any man can be considered as a member of Civil Society, he must be considered as a subject of the Governor of the Universe."

First chief justice of the U.S. Supreme Court, John Jay, wrote:

"Providence has given to our people the choice of their rulers, and it is the duty ... of our Christian nation to select and prefer Christians for their rulers." (1816)

Justice David Brewer said this:

"This is a religious people. This is historically true. From the discovery of this continent to the present hour, there is a single voice making this affirmation ... We find everywhere a clear recognition of the same truth ... These, and many other matters which might be noticed, add a volume of unofficial declarations to the mass of organic utterances that this is a Christian nation. (1892)

Even liberal Supreme Court chief justice, Earl Warren, wrote in 1954:

"I believe no one can read the history of our country without realizing that the Good Book and the spirit of the Savior have from the beginning been our guiding geniuses ... Whether we look to the first Charter of Virginia ... or to the Charter of New England ... or to the

Charter of Massachusetts Bay ... or to the Fundamental Orders of Connecticut ... the same objective is present ... a Christian land governed by Christian principles. I believe the entire Bill of Rights came into being because of the knowledge our forefathers had of the Bible and their belief in it: freedom of belief, of expression, of assembly, of petition, the dignity of the individual, the sanctity of the home, equal justice under law, and the reservation of powers to the people ... I like to believe we are living today in the spirit of the Christian religion. I like also to believe that as long as we do so, no great harm can come to our country."

Supreme Court justices were certainly not the only political figures who wrote such things either.

Roger Sherman:

"... all civil rights and the right to hold office were to be extended to persons of any Christian denomination."

John Quincy Adams:

"The greatest glory of the American Revolution was this: It connected in one indissoluble bond, the principles of civil government with the principles of Christianity."

"No book in the world deserves to be so unceasingly studied, and so profoundly meditated upon as the Bible."

"Is it not that the Declaration of Independence first organized the social compact on the Foundation of the Redeemer's mission upon earth? That it laid the cornerstone of human government upon the first precepts of Christianity?"

Abraham Lincoln:

"Unless the great God who assisted [President Washington], shall be with me and aid me, I must fail. But if the same omniscient mind, and Almighty arm, that directed and protected him, shall guide and support me, I shall not fail ... Let us pray that the God of our fathers may not forsake us now."

Grover Cleveland:

"All must admit that the reception of the teachings of Christ results in the purest patriotism, in the most scrupulous fidelity to public trust, and in the best type of citizenship."

Teddy Roosevelt:

"In this actual world, a churchless community, a community where men have

abandoned and scoffed at, or ignored their religious needs, is a community on the rapid down-grade."

Woodrow Wilson:

"America was born a Christian nation. America was born to exemplify that devotion to the elements of righteousness which are derived from the revelations of the Holy Scripture."

Calvin Coolidge, speaking of the founding fathers:

"They were intent upon establishing a Christian commonwealth in accordance with the principle of self-government. They were an inspired body of men. It has been said that God sifted the nations that He might send choice grain into the wilderness ... Who can fail to see it in the hand of Destiny? Who can doubt that it has been guided by a Divine Providence?"

John F. Kennedy:

"The rights of man come not from the generosity of the state but from the hand of God."

Gerald Ford, quoted a speech made by Dwight Eisenhower in 1955:

"Without God there could be no American form of government, nor an American way of life. Recognition of the Supreme Being is the first--the most basic--expression of Americanism. Thus, the founding fathers of America saw it, and thus with God's help, it will continue to be."

Quotes from www.learnreligions.com

*****AMERICA'S SOUL*****

God will judge our nation if we continue to allow this deceit – just as he judged the people before the flood and Sodom and Gomorrah! I don't think anyone can dispute that we are a Christian nation – Even a president! If you need more – study (some people prefer to be willfully ignorant). I think it all started when we took bibles out of school. When I was in grade school, we went next door to the church once a week for bible study. We need to reinstate bible study in schools. Get back to our roots. Bring back America's soul, as Joe says.

Proverbs 22:6 - Train up a child in the way he should go: and when he is old, he will not depart from it.

2 Peter 3:9 - The Lord is not slack

concerning his promise, as some men count slackness; but is longsuffering to us-ward, not willing that any should perish, but that all should come to repentance.

Our greatest enemy is the Devil himself. The Bible talks about the wiles of the Devil. Those who are not God's children can easily be used by him. God wants us to come to him.

Mark 10:14 - "Let the children come to me, for the Kingdom of God belongs to such as they. Don't send them away! I tell you as seriously as I know how that anyone who refuses to come to God as a little child will never be allowed into his Kingdom."

He wants us to come to him as innocents, as little children, with their great way of being a sponge. Grab his love and believe with a simple faith. He gave us a great intelligent, so we can learn about him, but we come as a child. Therefore, we become his child spiritually. With blind faith, as a small child trusts his parent to not bring him harm. We begin to have a great hunger to know him better. We read his word and learn about him. But don't forget your first love – him. Many will try to sway you into great rabbit trails that take you away. However, the more you study, the more you find that all these trails lead back to your Daddy.

1 Peter 5:8 - Be sober, be vigilant; because your adversary the devil, as a roaring lion, walketh about, seeking whom he may devour: Whom resist stedfast in the faith, knowing that the same afflictions are accomplished in your brethren that are in the world. But the God of all grace,

who hath called us unto his eternal glory by Christ Jesus, after that ye have suffered a while, make you perfect, stablish, strengthen, settle you.

2 Corinthians 4:3 - If the Good News we preach is hidden to anyone, it is hidden from the one who is on the road to eternal death. Satan, who is the god of this evil world, has made him blind, unable to see the glorious light of the Gospel that is shining upon him or to understand the amazing message we preach about the glory of Christ, who is God.

It is easy to follow the devil – but difficult to follow God. Following the devil takes no effort on your part – just do what you want – anything goes. The Devil does not care what you do – the worse you are the better. He wants you as far from God as possible. It's like there is a great contest between the two. Read Job.

Following God – well, that's a horse of a different color.

Matthew 7:13-14 - Enter ye in at the strait gate: for wide is the gate, and broad is the way, that leadeth to destruction, and many there be which go in thereat: Because strait is the gate, and narrow is the way, which leadeth unto life, and few there be that find it.

Few find it because it takes thought and hard work. Most people stumble thru their life with little thought to what comes after. But our fight is not of this world:

Ephesians 6:10 - Put on the whole armour of God, that ye may be able to stand against the wiles of the devil. For

we wrestle not against flesh and blood, but against principalities, against powers, against the rulers of the darkness of this world, against spiritual wickedness in high places. Wherefore take unto you the whole armour of God, that ye may be able to withstand in the evil day, and having done all, to stand. Stand therefore, having your loins girt about with truth, and having on the breastplate of righteousness; And your feet shod with the preparation of the gospel of peace; Above all, taking the shield of faith, wherewith ye shall be able to quench all the fiery darts of the wicked. And take the helmet of salvation, and the sword of the Spirit, which is the word of God.

We are in a spiritual battle for our souls – God wants us and will call each of us. But he does not want a bunch of robots. He gives us free will, so we can choose what we want and how to live our lives. He will never override our will. He WANTS us to choose him – but he will not make us love him and follow him.

Revelation 22:17 - And the Spirit and the bride say, Come. And let him that heareth say, Come. And let him that is athirst come. And whosoever (there it is again!) will, let him take the water of life freely.

As a new Christian – you will be like a baby – drinking milk – not eating meat. You will be very thirsty for God's word. This is why it is so important you surround yourself with Godly people and attend a Godly church.

John 7:37 - "If anyone is thirsty, let him come to me and drink. For the Scriptures declare that rivers of living water shall

flow from the inmost being of anyone who believes in me."

Matthew 5:6 - Blessed are they which do hunger and thirst after righteousness: for they shall be filled.

Beware: The Devil seeks to destroy you. He will pull very hard to get you to turn from God – or to pervert his word.

Isaiah 5:20 - Woe unto them that call evil good, and good evil; that put darkness for light, and light for darkness; that put bitter for sweet, and sweet for bitter!

Woe unto them that are wise in their own eyes, and prudent in their own sight! Woe unto them that are mighty to drink wine, and men of strength to mingle strong drink:

Which justify the wicked for reward, and

take away the righteousness of the righteous from him! Therefore as the fire devoureth the stubble, and the flame consumeth the chaff, so their root shall be as rottenness, and their blossom shall go up as dust: because they have cast away the law of the lord of hosts, and despised the word of the Holy One of Israel.

Isaiah 29:15 - Woe to those who try to hide their plans from God, who try to keep him in the dark concerning what they do! "God can't see us," they say to themselves. "He doesn't know what is going on!" How stupid can they be! Isn't he, the Potter, greater than you, the jars he makes? Will you say to him, "He didn't make us"? Does a machine call its inventor dumb?

Today there are even pastors, Christian

leaders and Christians perverting the word of God. They will be turned away by God:

Matthew 7:22-24 - Many will say to me in that day, Lord, Lord, have we not prophesied in thy name? and in thy name have cast out devils? and in thy name done many wonderful works? And then will I profess unto them, I never knew you: depart from me, ye that work iniquity.

Matthew 23:27 - Woe unto you, scribes and Pharisees, hypocrites! for ye are like unto whited sepulchres, which indeed appear beautiful outward, but are within full of dead men's bones, and of all uncleanness.

Even so ye also outwardly appear righteous unto men, but within ye are full of hypocrisy and iniquity.

Hosea 7:13 - Woe to my people for deserting me; let them perish, for they have sinned against me. I wanted to redeem them but their hard hearts would not accept the truth.

Acts 20:28 - "And now beware! Be sure that you feed and shepherd God's flock— his church, purchased with his blood—for the Holy Spirit is holding you responsible as overseers. I know full well that after I leave you, false teachers, like vicious wolves, will appear among you, not sparing the flock. Some of you yourselves will distort the truth in order to draw a following. Watch out!

They are much like the Pharisees in the time of Christ – thinking they know more than God. But Jesus said they got their reward in this life – living godless lives and high on the hog – important in the sight of their peers – ignoring God's word, even though they know it.

Matthew 6:5 - And when thou prayest, thou shalt not be as the hypocrites are: for they love to pray standing in the synagogues and in the corners of the streets, that they may be seen of men. Verily I say unto you, They have their reward.

Matthew 6:6 - But thou, when thou prayest, enter into thy closet, and when thou hast shut thy door, pray to thy Father which is in secret; and thy Father which seeth in secret shall reward thee openly.

Study and you will find many more passages on this topic.

I pray as I write this that those who are being molested (as I was) and those engulfed in this lifestyle can have the courage to run!!! Those who are willing – face your sin and repent – turn away from it and turn to God. He is your refuge. Save your soul! I pray for the innocents being molested and encouraged toward this lifestyle. Find strength in God. Pray Pray Pray. Even in your days of despair and when you are helpless and being abused – God will draw near to you.

Hebrews 13:5 - Let your conversation be without covetousness; and be content with such things as ye have: for he hath said, I will never leave thee, nor forsake thee.

James 4:8 - Draw nigh to God, and he will draw nigh to you. Cleanse your hands, ye sinners; and purify your hearts, ye double minded.

James 1:21 - So get rid of all that is wrong in your life, both inside and outside, and humbly be glad for the wonderful message we have received, for it is able to save our souls as it takes hold of our hearts. And remember, it is a message to obey, not just to listen to. So don't fool yourselves. For if a person just listens and doesn't obey, he is like a man looking at his face in a mirror; as soon as he walks away, he can't see himself anymore or remember what he looks like. But if anyone keeps looking steadily into God's law for free men, he will not only remember it but he will do what it says, and God will greatly bless him in everything he does.

Hold onto to these truths and pray – he will rescue you. He will bring you out in a miraculous way.

So, here's the DEALEO — you will die soon (in cosmic time). Only YOU can decide if you want to spend eternity in Heaven or Hell. If Heaven – then get busy! There is NO escaping it. It will be one or the other.

You are mind, body and soul.

MIND: the mind is like your hard drive – where your thoughts and feelings are pro-cessed – where your precious memories are stored. Be very careful what you take in — Garbage in – Garbage out. Your mind cannot distinguish real from fake. When you witness evil on TV – it believes it to be real. This violence will desensitize you to evil – opening up a wide door for the devil. It is full of depravity. I have not had a TV in over 10 years. And people wonder why there is so much evil today!!! Duh! You take God away and fill their heads with violence – and your surprised?? Oh – "it's the guns" – how absurd.

BODY: very temporary. It is your temple. It is only a holding tank for your soul, while you are here to prove yourself.

1 Corinthians 6:19-20 - What? know ye not that your body is the temple of the Holy Ghost which is in you, which ye have of God, and ye are not your own? For ye are bought with a price: therefore glorify God in your body, and in your spirit, which are God's.

SOUL: Yes; only you can decide how you will spend eternity; however, God will judge you. The Bible very clearly spells out how you should live your life. You are being tested and molded to see if you will become the person God created you to be. We all have free will. But, God will not pursue you forever. If you should turn your back on him – he will turn his back on you. Guard your soul – it is eternal.

Romans 1:28 - And even as they did not like to retain God in their knowledge, God gave them over to a reprobate mind.....

Psalm 5:8 - Lord, lead me as you promised me you would; otherwise my enemies will conquer me. Tell me clearly what to do, which way to turn. For they cannot speak one truthful word. Their hearts are filled to the brim with wickedness. Their suggestions are full of the stench of sin and death. Their tongues are filled with flatteries to gain their wicked ends. O God, hold them responsible. Catch them in their own traps; let them fall beneath the weight of their own transgressions, for they rebel against you.

For God is all powerful and will judge you according to his own words – but he also loves you and is merciful and gracious.

Hebrews 10:31 - It is a fearful thing to fall into the hands of the living God.

You cannot justify sin. You cannot run from it. You cannot decide what sin is. Only God can. All you can do is to fall on your knees, confess your sins, repent from them and ask God for forgiveness. In his mercy, he will forgive you......but you better be sincere. God will not be mocked. It is not fair to expect others to embrace your sinful lifestyle – bake cakes – give Uber drives – allow offenders of God's word to teach in a Christion school (which I believe had to be a set up)! Get control of yourselves! Ask someone else to bake you a cake – or do it yourself!!! You need to accept their

"No" as their answer – and their right to it – just as you have your right to do as you wish. You cannot demand your rights and deny other's their rights – just because they disagree with you. It is still America! You cannot expect others to accept this deviant lifestyle!! They have rights also. Be humble – be respectful of others as you want them to be of you. You have every right to do as you wish – but just know that many actions have eternal effects! This life is but a whisper in time, and you will be meeting up with God before you know it!

2 Peter 1:10 - So, dear brothers, work hard to prove that you really are among those God has called and chosen, and then you will never stumble or fall away. And God will open wide the gates of heaven for you to enter into the eternal kingdom of our Lord and Savior Jesus Christ.

For after you die you will be held accountable for your life and the decisions you have made:

Romans 14:11 - For it is written, "As I live," says the Lord, "every knee shall bow to me and every tongue confess to God." Yes, each of us will give an account of himself to God.

We are all tempted in this life to error. We have to choose good over evil. It is a conscious choice. If you think back, you will remember when you made some of the choices you did. Be honest with yourself. Unfortunately, the devil is very crafty and can use others to persuade us. It takes a VERY strong person – especially in the younger years – to choose the right path. The deceivers may even be people in authority over you – in high places. But God gives you this advise:

Matthew 7:15 - "Beware of false teachers who come disguised as harmless sheep, but are wolves and will tear you apart. You can detect them by the way they act, just as you can identify a tree by its fruit. You need never confuse grapevines with thorn bushes or figs with thistles. Different kinds of fruit trees can quickly be identified by examining their fruit. A variety that produces delicious fruit never produces an inedible kind. And a tree producing an inedible kind can't produce what is good. So the trees having the inedible fruit are chopped down and thrown on the fire. Yes, the way to identify a tree or a person is by the kind of fruit produced.

Ephesians 6:10 - Last of all I want to remind you that your strength must come

from the Lord's mighty power within you. Put on all of God's armor so that you will be able to stand safe against all strategies and tricks of Satan. For we are not fighting against people made of flesh and blood, but against persons without bodies—the evil rulers of the unseen world, those mighty satanic beings and great evil princes of darkness who rule this world; and against huge numbers of wicked spirits in the spirit world.

Luke 17:1 - "There will always be temptations to sin," Jesus said one day to his disciples, "but woe to the man who does the tempting. If he were thrown into the sea with a huge rock tied to his neck, he would be far better off than facing the punishment in store for those who harm these little children's souls. I am warning you!

Job 17:12 - They say that night is day and day is night; how they pervert the truth!

Those who are subverting the word of God will be facing a terrible judgement – especially those professing to know him! How can you know him if you don't read his word? And how can you read his word and not know his heart and his standards? They are like today's fake news – they pick out bits and pieces out of context and try to sway people for their own agenda. They water down the word of God and let you believe it is OK to sin. Woe to them!!! God has their destiny in his word. I pray that they confess and turn to God.

John 8:44 - Jesus Says: Ye are of your father the devil, and the lusts of your father ye will do. He was a murderer from the beginning, and abode not in the truth,

because there is no truth in him. When he speaketh a lie, he speaketh of his own: for he is a liar, and the father of it.

And because I tell you the truth, ye believe me not.

Which of you convinceth me of sin? And if I say the truth, why do ye not believe me?

He that is of God heareth God's words: ye therefore hear them not, because ye are not of God.

2 Timothy 4:3 - For there is going to come a time when people won't listen to the truth but will go around looking for teachers who will tell them just what they want to hear. They won't listen to what the Bible says but will blithely follow their own misguided ideas.

No worries!!! God has made it very easy to come to him – your choice. I remember when I was baptized at 12 years old. I became a friend of God. We have been friends ever since. Like many friendships, we have had our ups and downs. There have been many times when we disagreed. There have been times when I was so angry, I refused to speak with him. Also, many times he punished me for my sins. But, I love him so much – I always come back and renew the closeness we enjoy. A friend told me they could never go to church because of all the hypocrites. I agree there are many. Actually, they are everywhere!!! Especially in every church. That is because Christ came for sinners not followers. It is where we learn about God. If you find a good church, it will be like a classroom – full of learning. Staying friends with God is a process. You start out taking baby steps – but eventually you will learn how to run!

Psalm 25:14 - Friendship with God is reserved for those who reverence him. With them alone he shares the secrets of his promises.

Psalm 54:4 - But God is my helper. He is a friend of mine!

Luke 12:8 - "And I assure you of this: I, the Messiah, will publicly honor you in the presence of God's angels if you publicly acknowledge me here on earth as your Friend.

Romans 5:10 - And since, when we were his enemies, we were brought back to God by the death of his Son, what blessings he must have for us now that we are his friends and he is living within us!

Now we rejoice in our wonderful new relationship with God—all because of what our Lord Jesus Christ has done in dying for our sins—making us friends of God.

2 Corinthians 13:14 - May the grace of our Lord Jesus Christ be with you all. May God's love and the Holy Spirit's friendship be yours. Paul

Hebrews 9:24 - For Christ has entered into heaven itself to appear now before God as our Friend. It was not in the earthly place of worship that he did this, for that was merely a copy of the real temple in heaven.

James 2:23 - And the scripture was fulfilled which saith, Abraham believed God, and it was imputed unto him for righteousness: and he was called the Friend of God.

Remember, if you accept Jesus and the father as your friends, you can expect their opinions to be known to you, in one way or another. God will correct us and let us know his opinion – if we will only listen. There are always consequences to every action.

Proverbs 3:11 - My son, despise not the chastening of the lord; neither be weary of his correction:

For whom the lord loveth he correcteth; even as a father the son in whom he delighteth.

I pray that someday you can share this relationship with others, so that they come to love the LORD. Let your light shine. Partner with someone who can share this journey with you. Attend study groups. Read your Bible daily. If you do not have a Bible, many churches will provide you with one. Of course, you can study online also.

2 Timothy 4 - I charge thee therefore before God, and the Lord Jesus Christ, who shall judge the quick and the dead at his appearing and his kingdom;

Preach the word; be instant in season, out of season; reprove, rebuke, exhort with all long suffering and doctrine.

For the time will come when they will not endure sound doctrine; but after their own lusts shall they heap to themselves teachers, having itching ears;

And they shall turn away their ears from the truth, and shall be turned unto fables.

There are people who do not believe the word of God. They say it is full of myths. I say they just have not studied.

Matthew 9:10 - And it came to pass, as Jesus sat at meat in the house, behold, many publicans and sinners came and sat down with him and his disciples. And when the Pharisees saw it, they said unto his disciples, Why eateth your Master with publicans and sinners? But when Jesus heard that, he said unto them, They that be whole need not a physician, but they that are sick. But go ye and learn what that meaneth, I will have mercy, and not sacrifice: for I am not come to call the righteous, but sinners to repentance.

1 John 1:5 - This is the message God has given us to pass on to you: that God is Light and in him is no darkness at all. So if we say we are his friends but go on living in spiritual darkness and sin, we are lying.

But if we are living in the light of God's presence, just as Christ does, then we have wonderful fellowship and joy with each other, and the blood of Jesus his Son cleanses us from every sin.

If we say that we have no sin, we are only fooling ourselves and refusing to accept the truth. But if we confess our sins to him, he can be depended on to forgive us and to cleanse us from every wrong. And it is perfectly proper for God to do this for us because Christ died to wash away our sins. If we claim we have not sinned, we are lying and calling God a liar, for he says we have sinned.

Matthew 13:47 - "Again, the Kingdom of Heaven can be illustrated by a fisherman—he casts a net into the water and gathers in fish of every kind, valuable and worthless. When the net is full, he drags it up onto the beach and sits down and sorts out the edible ones into crates and throws the others away. That is the way it will be at the end of the world—the angels will come and separate the wicked people from the godly, casting the wicked into the fire; there shall be weeping and gnashing of teeth. Do you understand?"

1 Corinthians 5:9 - When I wrote to you before I said not to mix with evil people. But when I said that I wasn't talking about unbelievers who live in sexual sin or are greedy cheats and thieves and idol worshipers. For you can't live in this world without being with people like that. What I meant was that you are not to keep company with anyone who claims to be a brother Christian but indulges in sexual sins, or is greedy, or is a swindler, or

worships idols, or is a drunkard, or abusive. Don't even eat lunch with such a person.

It isn't our job to judge outsiders. But it certainly is our job to judge and deal strongly with those who are members of the church and who are sinning in these ways. God alone is the Judge of those on the outside. But you yourselves must deal with this man and put him out of your church.

Why do we go to church? To hear God's word. If you are becoming – searching for the truth – thirsty – hungry – your soul will be fed in church – a good Bible church. Unfortunately, a lot of them today are not.

Romans 10:8 - For salvation that comes from trusting Christ—which is what we preach—is already within easy reach of each of us; in fact, it is as near as our own hearts and mouths. For if you tell others with your own mouth that Jesus Christ is your Lord and believe in your own heart that God has raised him from the dead, you will be saved. For it is by believing in his heart that a man becomes right with God; and with his mouth he tells others of his faith, confirming his salvation.

For the Scriptures tell us that no one who believes in Christ will ever be disappointed. Jew and Gentile are the same in this respect: they all have the same Lord who generously gives his riches to all those who ask him for them. Anyone who calls upon the name of the Lord will be saved.

But how shall they ask him to save them unless they believe in him? And how can they believe in him if they have never heard about him? And how can they hear about him unless someone tells them? And how will anyone go and tell them unless someone sends him? That is what the Scriptures are talking about when they say, "How beautiful are the feet of those who preach the Gospel of peace with God and bring glad tidings of good things." In other words, how welcome are those who come preaching God's Good News!

But not everyone who hears the Good News has welcomed it, for Isaiah the prophet said, "Lord, who has believed me when I told them?" Yet faith comes from listening to this Good News—the Good News about Christ.

We are all sinners, even some of the major players in the Bible sinned against God:

King David: He was an adulterer and a murderer. They were at war. He lusted after Bathsheba and committed adultery with her. When he found out she was pregnant, he called her husband back from the battle and tried to get him to sleep with her to hide the crime – but Uriah (her husband) refused and slept on the front stoop. When King David asked him why – he said he could not enjoy his wife when all his minions were at the battle fighting. Stage left – he had her husband killed and married Bathsheba. No one knew, but God did – (he sent a prophet) - she lost the babe. However, God said King David was a man after his own heart!

2 Samuel 11 - In the spring of the following year, at the time when wars begin, David sent Joab and the Israeli army to destroy the Ammonites. They began by

laying siege to the city of Rabbah. But David stayed in Jerusalem.

One night he couldn't get to sleep, and went for a stroll on the roof of the palace. As he looked out over the city, he noticed a woman of unusual beauty taking her evening bath. He sent to find out who she was and was told that she was Bathsheba, the daughter of Eliam and the wife of Uriah. Then David sent for her and when she came he slept with her.................

Read the rest of it!!! It's a great story and example of God's mercy and love.

Abraham was an idolater, deceiver and adulterer – but God tested him and he became the father of the greatest nation in the world – Israel! God will test you – to see where your heart is. When you are faced with a decision – do not act rashly

– give grave consideration to every decision you make.

Genesis 22:1 - Later on, God tested Abraham's faith and obedience. "Abraham!" God called. "Yes, Lord?" he replied. "Take with you your only son— yes, Isaac whom you love so much—and go to the land of Moriah and sacrifice him there as a burnt offering upon one of the mountains which I'll point out to you!" The next morning Abraham got up early, chopped wood for a fire upon the altar, saddled his donkey, and took with him his son Isaac and two young men who were his servants, and started off to the place where God had told him to go. On the third day of the journey Abraham saw the place in the distance.

"Stay here with the donkey," Abraham

told the young men, "and the lad and I will travel yonder and worship, and then come right back."

Abraham placed the wood for the burnt offering upon Isaac's shoulders, while he himself carried the knife and the flint for striking a fire. So the two of them went on together.

"Father," Isaac asked, "we have the wood and the flint to make the fire, but where is the lamb for the sacrifice?"

"God will see to it, my son," Abraham replied. And they went on.

When they arrived at the place where God had told Abraham to go, he built an altar and placed the wood in order, ready for the fire, and then tied Isaac and laid him on the altar over the wood. And Abraham took the knife and lifted it up to plunge it into his son, to slay him.

At that moment the Angel of God shouted to him from heaven, "Abraham! Abraham!"

"Yes, Lord!" he answered.

"Lay down the knife; don't hurt the lad in any way," the Angel said, "for I know that God is first in your life—you have not withheld even your beloved son from me."

Then Abraham noticed a ram caught by its horns in a bush. So he took the ram and sacrificed it, instead of his son, as a burnt offering on the altar. Abraham named the place "Jehovah provides"—and it still goes by that name to this day.

Then the Angel of God called again to

Abraham from heaven. "I, the Lord, have sworn by myself that because you have obeyed me and have not withheld even your beloved son from me, I will bless you with incredible blessings and multiply your descendants into countless thousands and millions, like the stars above you in the sky, and like the sands along the seashore. They will conquer their enemies, and your offspring will be a blessing to all the nations of the earth—all because you have obeyed me."

Saul was an Israeli official – commissioned with capturing and killing the Christians. Until Jesus got his attention on the road to Damascus: read the full chapter. God changed his name to Paul and he became a mighty witness. He is the reason the gospel was spread to us gentiles!!!

Acts 9:1 - And Saul, yet breathing out threatenings and slaughter against the disciples of the Lord, went unto the high priest, And desired of him letters to Damascus to the synagogues, that if he found any of this way, whether they were men or women, he might bring them bound unto Jerusalem. And as he journeyed, he came near Damascus: and suddenly there shined round about him a light from heaven:

Study!!!!

There are many more examples in the Bible.

John Starnes has a song I love: "If God could only use perfect people, he could not use anyone at all". Ain't it de truth!!!!

Romans 3:23 – for all have sinned and

come short of the glory of the LORD.

James 2:10 – for whosoever (there it is again! I love that word!) shall keep the whole law, and just offend in one part, he is guilty of all.

Wow once again!!! God has really leveled the playing field. No one is any better than the other. If you have lied, or stolen something, etc. — you are just as guilty as the mass murderer in prison that is seeking God's grace! It really humbles you when you see yourself thru God's eyes.

We all come with shame and guilt. You ask: "How could God want me – or care about me? If I ever stepped thru the church door, the building would be struck by lightning and it would be burned to the ground! You could not be more wrong!

Remember this: Jesus is your brother and wants to be your best friend. Our Father (who art in Heaven) loves us with a love so great we can never fathom it's depth. Only in Heaven will we know how much he has grieved for us.

God will tug on your heart strings at some-time in your life – for some it takes many times. When you hear his voice in your spirit — LISTEN! He is calling you into his family. His child........ Your choice.

So – the greatest gift of all:

Romans 8:17 – And if children, then being heirs of GOD, and joint heirs with Christ; if so be that we suffer with him, that we may also be glorified together.

Wow!!! Joint heirs with Christ. What a prize we win! But remember this is not something we can earn. It is a free gift from God.

This means that God is very patient with us – but as I said before, he will not beg us. He does not want any of us to be lost.

2 Chronicles 16:9 - For the eyes of the Lord search back and forth across the whole earth, looking for people whose hearts are perfect toward him, so that he can show his great power in helping them.

Ephesians 2:8-9 - For by grace are ye saved through faith; and that not of yourselves: it is the gift of God: Not of works, lest any man should boast.

How merciful is God!! He knows how prideful we all are. But he brings us all down to the dust we are made of. There is not a thing you can do to win God's love

— it is a free gift! We come to God in the same way – we recognize that we are a sinner – and call out for him to save us from ourselves. He is willing to love us just as we are. You come to him with all your sin as baggage. His grace will cover all your sins and forgive you. No matter what your past!!! Once you come sincerely to God and walk away from your sins, you become a new person. You start to hunger for his word and his will. God will send you the Holy Spirit. He becomes your conscience and will guide you if you will listen. My own opinion – I believe this is why there is so much evil in our world today – people commit such dastardly deeds! I believe it is because they have turned their backs on God & the Holy Spirit does not reside in them. They have accepted the devil – becoming willingly ignorant. Their conscience is seared.

These are our levels of competence:

Unconscious – Incompetence: you lack knowledge, but are not aware of it.

Conscious – Incompetence: you lack knowledge, but are aware of your ignorance.

Conscious – competence: you have knowledge and think and plan an action.

Unconscious – Competence: you have the knowledge and do not have to think and plan an action. You just do.

How blessed it is to be unconsciously competent in your relationship with God!

Ephesians 3:14 - When I think of the wisdom and scope of his plan, I fall down on my knees and pray to the Father of all the great family of God—some of them

already in heaven and some down here on earth— that out of his glorious, unlimited resources he will give you the mighty inner strengthening of his Holy Spirit. And I pray that Christ will be more and more at home in your hearts, living within you as you trust in him. May your roots go down deep into the soil of God's marvelous love; and may you be able to feel and understand, as all God's children should, how long, how wide, how deep, and how high his love really is; and to experience this love for yourselves, though it is so great that you will never see the end of it or fully know or understand it. And so at last you will be filled up with God himself.

Now glory be to God, who by his mighty power at work within us is able to do far more than we would ever dare to ask or even dream of—infinitely beyond our

highest prayers, desires, thoughts, or hopes. May he be given glory forever and ever through endless ages because of his master plan of salvation for the Church through Jesus Christ.

Martin Luther King Jr. said: "Nothing in all the world is more dangerous than sincere ignorance and conscious stupidity."

John Wooden: "Without proper self-evaluation, Failure is inevitable."

Many people will try to dissuade you and laugh when you tell them that God has pulled on your heart:

2 Peter 3:3 – knowing this first, that there shall come in the last days scoffers, walking after their own lusts, and saying, where is the promise of his coming? For since the fathers fell asleep, all things continue

as they were from the beginning of creation. (read more of this)

Many people look for reasons to justify their sin. They will lie to you and do anything they can to turn you away from God. Don't let them. Don't drink the Koolaid!!! You may need to make some serious changes in your life to follow Christ. No one said it would be easy. We all have our vices as sinners. We all have a cross to bear. No one is exempt.

Matthew 16:24 - Then Jesus said to the disciples, "If anyone wants to be a follower of mine, let him deny himself and take up his cross and follow me. For anyone who keeps his life for himself shall lose it; and anyone who loses his life for me shall find it again. What profit is there if you gain the whole world—and lose eternal life?

What can be compared with the value of eternal life? For I, the Son of Mankind, shall come with my angels in the glory of my Father and judge each person according to his deeds.

This is why - the road is narrow. Attend a Bible believing church and confess your sins. This act will take a big weight off your shoulders and bring you closer to God.

James 5:16 - Confess your faults one to another, and pray one for another, that ye may be healed. The effectual fervent prayer of a righteous man availeth much.

Be thankful for those saints that are praying for you. This may be the calling that you need. Heed the call.

There is great rejoicing in Heaven when someone is saved:

Juke 15:3 - So Jesus used this illustration: "If you had a hundred sheep and one of them strayed away and was lost in the wilderness, wouldn't you leave the ninety-nine others to go and search for the lost one until you found it? And then you would joyfully carry it home on your shoulders. When you arrived you would call together your friends and neighbors to rejoice with you because your lost sheep was found.

"Well, in the same way heaven will be happier over one lost sinner who returns to God than over ninety-nine others who haven't strayed away!

Listen to Cory Asbury's song – "Reckless Love"

Luke 15:10 - In the same way there is joy in the presence of the angels of God when

one sinner repents.

Our pastor at Emmanuel Church in Greenwood, Ind. Recently gave a sermon that really hit home. He was talking about the choices we make and how through-out our lives we can stray from God and widen the gap between us. He said there are 3 main things we need to do to stay close to him:

Read the Bible daily and study it

Surround yourself with Godly people

Listen to Gospel music

All three of these I find crucial in my walk with God. I could not be happy if either of them were lost to me. I think of my daughter signing to songs at church. How the deaf enjoy God's music. God is the in-ventor of music – to be used for worship.

Unfortunately, a lot of music today is not uplifting – even down right in the gutter. Your spirit will tell you if you will listen, that this is not good for your soul. Through music, God calls to us. Our spirits are lifted up and we worship God.

James 4:7 - So give yourselves humbly to God. Resist the devil and he will flee from you. And when you draw close to God, God will draw close to you. Wash your hands, you sinners, and let your hearts be filled with God alone to make them pure and true to him. Let there be tears for the wrong things you have done. Let there be sorrow and sincere grief. Let there be sadness instead of laughter, and gloom instead of joy. Then when you realize your worthlessness before the Lord, he will lift you up, encourage and help you.

I have found that God has answered my prayers in strange ways sometimes. He has a great since of humor and will guide you in ways you could never imagine. He will put people in your life and orchestrate events to your good, if only you trust in him.

Romans 8:26 - And in the same way—by our faith —the Holy Spirit helps us with our daily problems and in our praying. For we don't even know what we should pray for, nor how to pray as we should, but the Holy Spirit prays for us with such feeling that it cannot be expressed in words. And the Father who knows all hearts knows, of course, what the Spirit is saying as he pleads for us in harmony with God's own will. And we know that all that happens to us is working for our good if we love God and are fitting into his plans.

So, our Father that loves us will turn evil to good for us, IF we are his child. If someone hurts us, he will fight the battle on our behalf and bring us to a better place.

I once worked for a large local builder in the area selling new homes in a model home. I loved my job very much, however, my manager and I were wrongfully fired.

I was very upset – but I knew that "vengeance is mine saithe the LORD", so I turned my anger and resentment over to God. Do you know a few months later I won a contest they were having and drove a new Pontiac Solstice (the first one in Indiana) out of that conference room and they wrote a $20,000 check for me to have that car for 2 years. Point is, leave your troubles to God and he will open doors you cannot even imagine. This does not mean you don't keep on keepin' on. You are responsible for yourself and your future.

Don't listen to that ole devil whispering in you ear that you are not good enough – God loves you.

My desire in writing this book is that God's word will soak into your soul. If just one person is added to our family, I will be satisfied. You're gonna die – BUT you will live forever – you need to choose where. Your death will be a fork in the road — you need to decide now which path to take. It will be too late then. Only you can choose where you want to spend eternity. I pray all who read this will turn away from their deadly lifestyle – (all sins) - and turn towards God.

Pray for God to come into your life. Pray:

"Dear God, I am a terrible sinner. I am sooo sorry for the terrible things I have done. I have gone against you. I believe that you sent your son, Jesus Christ, to die for me, to be buried and to deny death and be resurrected for our sins. I am turning my life over to you. I have messed it up so bad — I know you can do better with what time I have left. I am turning my back on sin and from now on, I will seek your word and your love. Please send me your Holy Spirit to guide my mind and heart. Direct my path."

Tell a friend what you have done and get to Church!!! I wish you all could come to Emmanuel – but they do have services on-line as many churches do. https://www.eclife.org You can listen to current and past sermons.

One of my favorite things to do, is to pick

a city and a church and listen to their sermon online. You can go to church in just about any city today!

I have found www.biblegateway.com to be a wonderful resource. You can listen to different versions of the Bible & look up any word and read all the passages containing that word.

I wish you God's speed — You have an invitation — now make your reservation — so you will know your destination — and I hope that someday we can go on a walkabout on those streets of gold in Heaven - together!!!! God Bless!!

**** P.S.: Be sure to study the Mark of the Beast!!****

Bible passages are from The King James version and The Living Bible.

Printed in the USA
CPSIA information can be obtained
at www.ICGtesting.com
LVHW022030031223
765564LV00016B/2157